More Advance Praise

"*The Secret Rules of Social Networking* is a helpful tool for understanding the dos, don'ts, and ways to stay safe when using social networking sites such as FaceBook, Instagram, as well as gaming and dating sites. The book is geared towards teens and young adults, especially those who may have difficulty understanding social rules, such as individuals with autism spectrum disorder. The book explains appropriate levels of sharing, safely using online sites, cyberbullying, and online relationships. For readers who have difficulty navigating this complex online environment, this will be a great resource as it explicitly states the rules in a clear and concise format. Finally, the book is an excellent teaching tool for parents, teachers, and counselors to promote safety and success online."

> – Shelley Viles, director, Center for Autism Spectrum Disorders Training, Antioch University New England

"This book does an awesome job of explaining social networking in a highly systemized and honest way. It almost reads like a flow chart, which makes confusing information a lot less confusing. Klipper and Shapiro-Rieser have not skirted any of the hard or scary issues, opening the door for some good, frank discussion. I recommend this book to anyone who has ever been confused by a social interaction in real time or online. Actually, I would recommend it to anyone who uses the Internet to communicate, ever."

> – Kari Dunn Buron, author of *A 5 Is Against the Law!*

D1398657

THE SECRET RULES OF SOCIAL NETWORKING

Barbara Klipper and
Rhonda Shapiro-Rieser

Illustrations by Yasmin Bahrami

AAPC
PUBLISHING

11209 Strang Line Rd.
Lenexa, Kansas 66215
www.aapcpublishing.net

©2015 AAPC Publishing
11209 Strang Line Rd.
Lenexa, Kansas 66215
www.aapcpublishing.net

Publisher's Cataloging-in-Publication

Klipper, Barbara.
    The secret rules of social networking / Barbara Klipper and Rhonda Shapiro-Rieser ; illustrations by Yasmin Bahrami. -- Shawnee Mission, Kansas : AAPC Publishing, [2015]

        pages ; cm.

        ISBN: 978-1-942197-02-7
        LCCN: 2015933482
        Summary: Advice on acceptable online behavior and etiquette for adolescents and young adults who have challenges with social skills, including social boundaries and friendships.--Publisher.

        1. Online social networks--Handbooks, manuals, etc. 2. Online social networks--Safety measures--Handbooks, manuals, etc. 3. Online etiquette--Handbooks, manuals, etc. 4. Social media--Handbooks, manuals, etc. 5. Online dating--Handbooks, manuals, etc. 6. Internet--Social aspects--Handbooks, manuals, etc. 7. Interpersonal relations in children--Juvenile literature. 8. Interpersonal relations in adolescence--Juvenile literature. 9. Youth--Sexual behavior--Juvenile literature. 10. Internet and children--Juvenile literature. 11. Internet and teenagers--Juvenile literature. 12. Internet--Safety measures--Juvenile literature. 13. Facebook (Firm)--Handbooks, manuals, etc. 14. Twitter (Firm)--Handbooks, manuals, etc. 15. Linkedin (Firm)--Handbooks, manuals, etc. 16. Instagram (Firm)--Handbooks, manuals, etc. 17. [Online social networks. 18. Online social networks--Safety measures. 19. Online etiquette. 20. Social media. 21. Online dating. 22. Internet--Social aspects. 23. Interpersonal relations. 24. Youth--Sexual behavior. 25. Internet--Safety measures. 26. Facebook (Firm) 27. Twitter (Firm) 28. Linkedin (Firm) 29. Instagram (Firm)] I. Shapiro-Rieser, Rhonda. II. Bahrami, Yasmin. III. Title.

HM742 .K55 2015
302.3/0285--dc23   1504

Background art behind illustrations: ©iStockphoto; www.istockphoto.com
This book is designed in Myriad Pro.

Printed in the United States of America.

DEDICATION

For all of my boys and my girl …
Rhonda Shapiro-Rieser

For everybody who wishes they knew the "rules" …
Barbara Klipper

TABLE OF CONTENTS

INTRODUCTION

- Have you tried to use sites like Facebook, Twitter, or LinkedIn and been uncomfortable because you didn't know how to start and keep online relationships?

- Have you ever communicated with someone in person or online and been told you shared too much or were annoying?

- Do you wonder why so many of your peers think that using technology to network socially is wonderful and why they spend so much time doing it?

- Do you spend most of your computer time gaming alone or with strangers because you can't figure out how to connect with people?

If you answered YES to any of these questions, this guide is for you. It is for people who have had problems because they're baffled by the social part of online social networking and for people who haven't tried online social networking but want to.

We think online social networking is a good thing. It can be a very good thing for a person with an autism spectrum disorder (ASD) or anyone else who has challenges in the realm of social skills. This is because interacting is a little easier online than it is in person. That is, you can communicate in your own way and at your own speed online, which you can't always do in person.

- Online social networking is a place where you can practice presenting your best self to the world.

- It's a wonderful place to practice your social skills with people who aren't part of your daily in-person life, so mistakes have fewer long-lasting consequences.

- You can control who interacts with you online. You can't always do that in person.

- You can "meet" lots of people who share your interests through social networking sites.

But there are also potential dangers in the online world, dangers you need to know about and understand if you want to have fun and stay safe while relating to people online. This guide was written to help you understand the secret rules of social networking, the ones you won't find in other books.

In order to understand the rules that guide online social networking, you first have to understand the social rules that guide in-person relationships. So we'll discuss those, too.

We wrote this guide for you, but we suggest that you share it with someone you trust, like a parent or teacher if you are a minor, or a counselor or social skills coach if you are an adult. You can ask that person to help you with anything we discuss that you don't understand.

The Internet is vast and wonderful. It allows you to find people who share your interests. It allows you to experiment and be creative. Whatever your passion or interest, there is a networking site for you. Here are a few examples.

- General sites like Facebook (facebook.com), Google+ (plus. google.com), or Tagged (tagged.com)

- Special interest sites like Elftown (elftown.com) for people who like fantasy and science fiction, and Gamer DNA (gamerdna.com), Cellufun (cellufun.com), and Raptr (raptr. com) for gamers

- Sites like Tumblr (tumblr.com) or Twitter (twitter.com) where you can post blogs or follow other bloggers

- Instagram (instagram.com) and similar sites where you can network around photos or videos that you upload

- LinkedIn (linkedin.com), which can help you network with people who work in your field

There are many more sites than we can list here, and they are being developed and changed all the time, so ask people you know in person or use your search engine to find the right site or sites for you.

You have control over how you present yourself to the people you interact with on these sites. You shouldn't lie, but you should share your best qualities. You don't need to write that you have agoraphobia or allergies, or are afraid of the dark. Through what you say about yourself and your responses to what others say, you can let others know you as a kind, caring, interesting individual. Everyone can use the Internet to create a community for themselves if they follow the social rules. Everyone. We promise.

Let's get started!

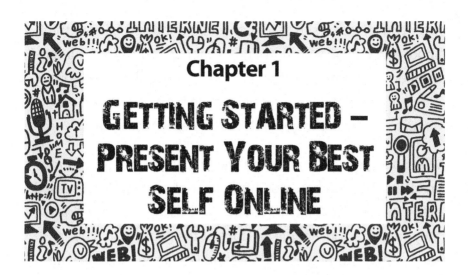

Chapter 1

GETTING STARTED – PRESENT YOUR BEST SELF ONLINE

Before you can make any online friends or share any information about yourself or your interests, you have to have an account on one or more social networking sites. You can pick a general site like Facebook or a site that caters to people with your special interest, like Elftown or Instagram. When picking sites to register with, look for ones that:

- Are free (be aware that some sites start out free but require payment later). If in-site purchases are available, make sure that you understand how to pay for them securely or discontinue them if you wish

- Protect the safety and privacy of members (for example, they have settings so you can decide who sees what)

- Seem easy to navigate and use. Well-run sites are clearly organized and provide user support if needed

After you choose a site to join, the next thing you have to think about is what you will show and say about yourself in your registration information and profile. Online sites all operate a little differently, and they frequently change how they work, so we are going to focus on the general ideas here, not the details.

When people meet you for the first time in person, they form an idea about you based on how you look and act. This is called a "first impression." First impressions are as important online as they are in person. People will look at the pictures you use and what you say about yourself to decide if they want to be your online friend, read your blog, or game with you. Also, employers may look at these things to help them decide whether to hire you. And people in the future may be able to see what you put on the Internet now, even if you think you deleted it. It is important to remember that in this way the Internet can be forever.

This leads us to the first rule of online social networking, which is: **PRESENT YOUR BEST SELF ONLINE.** Presenting your best self online starts with registration or creating your profile, depending on the site.

Registering

Choosing a Username and a Password

When you register, the site may ask you to create a username and pick a password. There are a few things to keep in mind when you do this.

1. Pick a username that represents your best self. For example, calling yourself "sexkitten1" will attract the wrong kind of attention. Gamergirl, for example, would be a better, less provocative choice if you want to network with other gamers.

2. Pick a username that is different from your email name. The more you vary things online, the safer you are.

3. The same goes for passwords. Don't use the same password for everything.

4. Don't share your passwords with anyone else, not even your best friends. (In the next chapter, we'll tell you how to know who are your best friends.)

5. Most sites have rules for passwords. They may need to be a certain length or contain a mix of letters and numbers. Follow your site's rules but stay away from using something that is easy for others to guess, like your birthday.

6. Write all of your usernames and passwords down and keep them in a safe place at home in case you forget them. Any place where you keep personal papers is a good choice, like your desk drawer if you have a desk. If you don't have a desk, pick a safe place in your room that you will remember. Your sock drawer is fine, for example.

Creating a Profile

The next thing you may have to do is create a profile. A profile is a short description of you. Different sites ask for different pieces of information as part of the profile. On many sites, you will be able to post a picture of yourself. There may also be questions to answer or a place to write a short biography. Some questions will be easy to answer, like "what is your birthday?" Others may be harder to answer, like "describe what you are like."

Here are some questions you might be asking about creating a profile:

• Do I have to tell the whole truth?

• If I don't like how I look, can I post someone else's picture or one I've doctored with Photoshop?

• Can I pretend to be another gender or a different age?

• Can I say I've been to college if I haven't?

The Internet is a wonderful place where imagination has no bounds and one can present oneself as almost anything. Many gamers have colleagues who present themselves as Orcs and Elves. That's fine in a game, but it is better to be your real self in your profile. You don't have to share everything (in fact, it is not good to share too much; we'll get into that later). But if you are interested in connecting with people online, you are more likely to find people you will enjoy interacting with if you are honest about who you are. So here are some guidelines to follow.

1. Pick a photograph that makes you look good but like yourself. Don't use the photo from your cousin's wedding. Pick one that looks like your everyday self, wearing nice clothes that you are comfortable in, like jeans and a tee shirt.

2. Don't use a photo that is sexually suggestive. For example, if you are a girl or woman, don't lean over and show your cleavage, don't pout or make kissing faces, and don't wear skimpy clothing. If you're a boy or a man, don't use a picture in which you are not wearing a shirt and your jeans are unzipped.

3. If you don't want to use a photo or don't have a suitable one, you can create an avatar and use that instead. An avatar is a cartoon-like representation of you. You can pick its hair color, clothes, and props. Some networking sites have internal features that allow you to create an avatar. There are also websites where you can create a free avatar that you can use on any social networking site. A few of these sites are Doopleme.com, Avachara.com, and reasonablyclever.com.

4. When you answer a question about what you like, list no more than three or four of your MAJOR interests. No one really needs to know that you like blue M&Ms the best.

5. If you list a relationship status, keep it simple ("single" or "in a relationship"). We'll talk more about your online relationship status in Chapter 6.

6. Remember, just because the site asks a question doesn't mean you have to answer it. For example, if you don't want to share your religion, your sexual orientation, or your politics, don't.

Now that you have an account and a profile, you're almost ready to start using your social networking site to find and connect with other people. But before we can talk about how to relate to people online, we need to talk a bit about friends in general. We'll spend the next chapter doing that.

Chapter 2

ABOUT FRIENDS

What are friends? You may know a lot of people, but they are not all friends. In general, someone is a friend if:

- You like them and they like you.

- They initiate contact with you as much as you initiate contact with them.

- They share secrets and possessions with you as much as you share with them.

- They are not mean to you.

Those are general guidelines, but if you think about it, you'll notice that all friends are not equal. There are different kinds of friends. Let us look at a few kinds. We'll start with the categories of what we'll call in-person friends. Then we'll move on to online friends.

Types of In-Person Friends

Best Friend: This is someone you've known for a long time. Your interests are similar, but you will listen to a best friend talk about something even when the subject isn't particularly interesting to you, at least for a little while. And a best friend will listen to you. You can count on him if you are in trouble, and he can count on you. You know each other's secrets and serious problems, and you can trust each other not to tell. Nobody has lots of best friends.

Good Friend: This is someone you like. You enjoy talking to her, and you like to do things together. You know some things about her life, but you don't share your secrets or your serious problems with her. You don't know her as well as a "best friend."

Gaming or Special Interest Buddy: This is someone you get together with to play games like *Magic,* or a person who shares your special interest. When you talk to each other, it's usually about the games you play or your common interests. You may even hang out a little, but you're always connected through the game or activity. You might not even know where this buddy lives, and you don't share your secrets or problems with him.

Acquaintance: Notice we didn't say "friend" or "buddy." Acquaintances are people you don't know very well. You may see them often, at school, at work, or at a store where you shop. You may know their names, and maybe you even like them. But they don't share much of themselves with you, and you don't share much about yourself either. Talk is about school or work or what you are buying, and you don't do anything socially together.

Friend of a Friend or Acquaintance: Sometimes you will meet friends of your friends or even friends of acquaintances. While there is the potential for them to become your friends, they are not your friends yet. Just because your friend trusts them, it doesn't mean you should.

To Review

Best Friends

- You feel safe talking to them. They know your secrets and other personal information, such as serious problems, and don't share them with others.

- You try to help them if they ask and you can trust them. If there is anyone you can call when you have a real emergency (like a serious medical problem or a flood in your apartment) at 3 a.m., it is a best friend.

- You have a lot of similar interests and values.

- You know a lot about them and they know a lot about you.

Good Friends

- You share some things but not the really personal things, like serious problems or secrets.

- You sometimes do things for them, and they sometimes do things for you.

- You have some similar interests and hang out around those interests.

Gaming or Special Interest Buddies

- You've met each other while playing games or through a shared interest.

- Your interactions are about games or shared activities.

- You don't know very much about their personal life. You may not even know where they live.

Acquaintances

- You don't know them very well.

- They don't share much about themselves with you.

- It is a relationship that doesn't go beyond the setting where you know them – school, work, or a business where you go on a regular basis.

- You'd say "hi" and maybe talk for two minutes or less about something simple like the weather if you see them in the supermarket.

Friends of Friends or Acquaintances

- You don't know very much about them except that someone else likes them.

- You have to wait and see if they want to get to know you better and if you want to get to know them better. While it may be tempting, you shouldn't trust them like a good friend or best friend until you get to know them better.

One way to illustrate all of this is to put people into a pyramid. The smallest section is for your best friends, and the largest area, at the bottom, is for friends of your friends or acquaintances. You'll notice that total strangers are not on the pyramid. Total strangers are people you may meet but you don't know anything about. You should not trust them or share personal information with them.

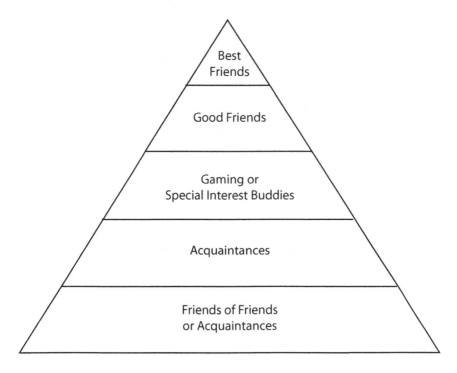

Online "Friends"

The first thing we need to do is to define the term "friend" when we are speaking about online relationships. In the online world, "friend" is a technical term that was coined by Facebook. It merely means someone you connect with on your social networking website. Some sites use other names, but the principle is the same. That's why a person can potentially have 400 online "friends" but not really know 350 of them. Who makes up the other 50? Two are best friends, 7 are good friends, 30 are acquaintances, 10 are gaming buddies, and 1 is their grandma. You may want to have a lot of online "friends," or you may want only a few. Either way is okay as long as you keep in mind the rules about what you share and who you trust.

A lot of what we said about in-person friends also applies to online friends. All of your in-person friend groups have the potential to be online friends also. If your in-person best friends, good friends, buddies, and acquaintances are registered with the same site as you, you can ask any of them to be "friends." You can also have online "friends" who are not friends in your daily in-person life. Sometimes social networking sites suggest people you might want to request to be "friends" with. These can be friends of your online friends, people who live in your community, people who share your interests, or people who went to your school. Sometimes people you don't know in person will send you a request via the site to become your "friend." We'll explain a bit more about how this process works in the next chapter.

Family Members

Some family members are people you are very close to; people you trust completely. All of the best friend rules apply to these members of your family.

Other family members (like the cousin who always teases you) are not people you should share a lot with online. It is okay to treat such people online like acquaintances, and it is also okay to not "friend" them at all. Remember, the family members you "friend" may be able to see everything you write on your page, and you may not want that.

If you are an adult, it is perfectly acceptable to ignore your mom's "friend" request if you don't want her to be part of your online life, even if you love and trust her. Your mom will still love you. If you are a minor, having your mom as a friend will allow her to help you monitor your online interactions and make sure they are appropriate.

Networking sites have privacy settings or something similar that allows you to control who sees what, even if they are a "friend." These settings can be helpful. But if you aren't sure what you can limit, it is better not to "friend" family members you don't trust or feel safe around, even if they send you a "friend" request.

Think of the relationship between your family and your online "friends" as presented in the following diagram.

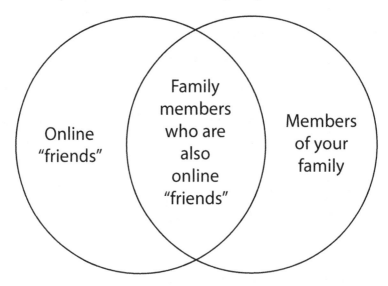

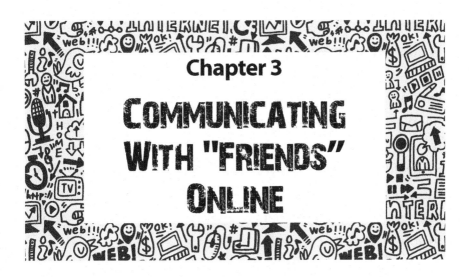

Chapter 3

COMMUNICATING WITH "FRIENDS" ONLINE

Now that you have an online account, and you know more about friends, what do you do next? You look for people to ask to be your online "friends," to be in your "circle," to "follow," or whatever these connections are called in the site you use. You may really, really want to start by looking up the name of the cute girl or guy who serves you coffee, but that is not the best place to start.

We'll get back to them later, but for now let's start with looking online for people you know. You can start with family members you like, gaming buddies, acquaintances from work or school, or your good or best in-person friends. If you find that one of these people is online, ask him to be your "friend" by sending a request (your online site will show you how to do this). You can send as many "friend" requests as you want. Some people approve all of these requests automatically. Others control whom they accept as "friends." This means that you may have to wait for a response to your request to connect or that some people may decide to ignore your request. You can do the same things with requests that you receive – approve them or ignore them.

Online Etiquette

This leads us to online etiquette. Here are some of the online etiquette rules (other people follow these and you can, too).

1. If someone doesn't approve your request, it means that they don't want to be your online "friend." This is tough but true. It happens to everyone. Repeated requests to the same person are annoying and will not help you gain approval. Move on to some-one else. This applies even if the person is an in-person friend.

2. If you say yes to someone's request, you can change your mind later and "unfriend" them. People can also do this to you. It is okay to do.

3. If someone asks you to be a "friend" and you aren't interested, it is okay to ignore the request.

4. You will have better success sending "friend" requests to people who know you. The cute person at the coffee shop may not know you nearly as well as you think you know her and may not respond to your request. It is not okay to mention this the next time you see her in person. This is a general rule … Don't make people uncomfortable by asking them why they didn't agree to be your online "friend." You probably wouldn't want someone you didn't like to make you uncomfortable by asking you that question.

Once you have some "friends," what's next?

Ways to Interact on a Social Networking Site

Let's look at some of the choices you have for interacting online.

Posting

On Facebook, for example, it is easy to look at what someone has written (these are called posts) and just click on the "like" button (different sites have different names for this feature, such as "favorite"). You don't have to write anything; your clicking lets the person know you are interested in what he or she has to say. This is a good way to start interacting online. Reading what other people are posting can help give you an idea of what they are interested in. It is also a great way to learn what kinds of posts are appropriate.

After you've "liked" someone's posts a few times, you can try posting a few things yourself. When you post, you write something in an allotted space that shows up on your online page. What you post can be seen by your online "friends" and by other people who look you up on the site.

Posting is public, so one way to start is with a simple statement about something new you've done that you want to tell others about.

 REMEMBER

Things that are okay to share include ...

- Cooking something new for dinner

- Seeing an interesting movie

- Reaching a high level in a game for the first time

- Hearing a new song by your favorite group

- Going on a trip

Things that are NOT okay to post include ...

- Everything you ate yesterday in detail

- The fact that you're on the computer (that's kind of obvious)

- Physical things, like the fact that you're constipated or have a bad zit

- The fact that you're doing something you're not supposed to do, like "I'm supposed to be at work but instead I stayed home to go online"

- Personal things about your family or other people you know, like the fact that your cousin failed math or your aunt is getting a divorce

- Information you have been asked to keep secret

You can also post about such topics as art, music, current events, or your hobby or special interest. Whether your posts are about your life or these topics, remember to always keep posts short, simple, and pleasant. For example, if you want to post about the fact that Cadbury Crème Eggs are not available all year, you can write a sentence saying that you are disappointed and wish you could buy enough candy eggs to last you until they go back on sale. You should not write a four-paragraph rant about the many ways that companies discontinue your favorite items and how corporations don't consider your needs or feelings.

Uploading Photos

Most general social networking sites allow you to upload photographs. Other sites like Instragram.com have been created specifically for photo sharing. In addition to posting (writing words to share), sharing photos is another way to introduce information about yourself and your interests online.

Many sites have a way that you can "tag" the people in the photos that you upload (this means labeling who is included in the picture). Remember, any photo you put online is available to the public, so here are the rules to follow:

- Don't put any photos on your online page that you wouldn't want your grandma to see (she may be online, too). Examples include photos that are sexually suggestive or photos that show something your grandma would disapprove of, like photos that show your messy room with clothes strewn all over.

- NEVER upload a photo of yourself in which you are naked. Don't let anyone convince you that this is okay, even as a joke. This is NEVER okay. It is against the law, and people have been arrested for doing it.

- Don't add other people's photos to your online page. It is up to them, not you, to decide if they want their pictures online. This includes pictures of your favorite celebrities.

- Make sure there is nothing in the background of your photo that is private or that would embarrass someone.

Sending Messages

There are a number of ways you can send messages to people on social networking sites. You may even be able to chat in real time. There are often ways to send private messages and other ways to send messages that will be seen by the public in addition to the person you are writing to. Make sure you know which you are doing before you send a message. For example, on Facebook a "message" is private, and a "comment" is public.

Here are some rules to follow when sending messages.

1. If you send someone private messages three times and they don't reply, it most likely means they don't want to communicate with you online. Stop sending them messages.

2. If someone is online, your chosen networking site may have a way of letting you know and a space on the webpage where you can chat with them. If you try to chat once with someone you know is online and the person doesn't respond, don't try to chat with him any more. He most likely does not want to talk to you or he is not interested in using the site's chat feature. If you keep trying, you might be annoying or even harassing that person. And as a result, he might decide to block your communications or "unfriend" you.

3. Don't mention anything personal or secret in messages that will be public.

4. If you want to comment on something someone has written, follow the rules we list later on in this chapter about how to communicate with different categories of friends.

REMEMBER

Be nice. Be polite. Don't be a jerk. If what you write is unpleasant, people may block your messages. They may "unfriend" you. Even if people don't block your messages or "unfriend" you, bad behavior could prevent you from creating online relationships with safe, trustworthy, kind people. Nice people do not want to be friends with jerks.

Other Things You Might Be Able to Do on a Networking Site

Ask People to Join a Group: These can be groups you create or groups you've joined. Groups consist of a subset of the members of a networking site who share a very specialized interest. For example, on a site for gamers, there might be a group for people who like a specific game.

Poll: Some sites let you poll people for their opinions on politics or popular culture or other topics.

Give Gifts: On some sites you can send people virtual gifts. These are not real items, just pictures of items that will appear on their page when you order them. Please note: There may be a fee associated with sending gifts.

Upload Your Creations: On some sites, you can upload videos you've made or art you've produced or things you've written for other people to comment on.

Poke: Facebook lets you "poke" people. When you "poke" someone, they get a message telling them they have been "poked." Poking can be a way to say "hi," or it can be a way to flirt with someone online; we'll get into that later on, in Chapter 6.

REMEMBER

If you do any of these things, the following social rules apply.

- What you post is public and FOREVER. Think before you upload. For example, do you really want a poem filled with obscene language and rants to represent you? Remember, nice people want to be friends with nice people. And years from now, when you feel differently about the topic, you may be embarrassed to know that people can still see the rant you wrote today.

- All of the rules for photos also apply to videos that you upload.

- Polling and poking are okay with best friends and good friends from time to time if your friends agree, but they can be annoying if you do them too much, just like they would be in person.

- Sending virtual gifts is okay, but if your friend doesn't respond in a positive way stop at one gift.

- You can send virtual gifts to best friends or good friends and also to people you want to flirt with, but only after you've read the rules about flirting in Chapter 5.

- Only send requests to join a group to best friends or good friends, with two exceptions:
  - If the group you create or join is about a special interest, you can send your special interest buddies an invitation to join.
  - You can invite colleagues who work in your field to join a work-related group with you on a site like LinkedIn.

So, now that you know some things you can do, how can you relate to your different groups of friends online? Here are the rules.

Best Friends

- You can "chat" with them if they also want to.

- You can send them private messages.

- You can send them virtual gifts, but only if they've responded positively to the first one.

- You can poll them – no more than once a week.

- You can invite them to join a group.

- You can "poke" them, but only if they say it is okay – no more than twice a week.

- You can tag them in photos.

- You can comment on things they post, but only say things you or they want others to see.

- You can "like" things they say or photos they post.

- You can play online games with them.

Good Friends

- You can chat with them if they also want to.

- You can send them private messages but not about secrets or problems.

- You can poll them – no more than twice a month.

- You can invite them to join groups.

- You can poke them – no more than twice a month.

- You can tag them in photos.

- You can comment on things they post.

- You can "like" things they say or photos they post.

- You can play online games with them.

Buddies

- You can chat with them if they also want to.

- You can comment on things they post that have to do with your common interests.

- You can invite them to join groups about your common interests.

- You can "like" things they say or photos they post.

- You can play online games with them.

Acquaintances

- You can "like" things they say or photos they post.

- You can comment on their posts, but only on things that have to do with your common interests.

- You can play online games with them.

Friends of Friends or Acquaintances

- You can "like" what they say or photos they post.

- You can comment on what they post but no more than once a week and only on things that have to do with your common interests.

- You can play online games with them.

Total Strangers

- You can play online games with them.

- You can chat with them during the game, but only about the game.

- If you find yourself playing a game with the same stranger more than five times, he or she becomes a gaming buddy, and the rules for relating to gaming buddies apply.

 REMEMBER

If an activity or behavior is not on the list, don't do it. If you're not sure, talk about it with the person with whom you are sharing this guide – a parent, teacher, counselor, or social skills coach.

Chapter 4

DANGER, DANGER . . . READ ALL ABOUT IT!

If you are following the rules from the earlier chapters, you have developed a presence in the online world. You have online "friends," and you know what and when to post to keep them. But there is more you need to know if you want to stay safe online. As we wrote earlier, the Internet is a wonderful place, but like many places in this world, there are some very dangerous neighborhoods.

We are going to give you guidelines for staying away from danger, both on social networking sites and other places online. There are predatory people online, people who lie and take advantage of other people. We'll spend part of this chapter telling you about some of the things that such people do online that can be hurtful. But if you know what to do to protect yourself, you can make sure that those people don't hurt YOU.

Here are the rules to follow to stay safe online.

Personal Information

1. Don't share personal identifying information in your profile or in posts, and don't share someone else's personal identifying information either. This is the first safety rule to follow.

2. Watch out for "phishing" – don't respond to pop-up messages or texts that ask for personal information. No legitimate business requests information that way.

For example …

- Never put your social security number, your bank account number, or your credit card number into any post or comment you make on an online social networking site. Never share this information with someone you meet online. Predatory people can use this information to steal your identity or your money.

- Don't post online that your entire family will be on vacation for two weeks. Burglars will know your house is empty and may come to rob you.

- Don't tell people you chat with online where you live. The town is okay, but don't give out your exact address.

- Be careful not to post photos that show your house number, your car's license plate, or other personal identifying information.

Some kinds of personal information are okay to share, like:

- Your hair or eye color

- Your birthday (in fact, some sites have automatic ways "friends" can send you "Happy Birthday" messages)

- Things you like and enjoy doing

This kind of personal information will help people get to know you and can't be used by predatory people to hurt you.

Money and Possessions

1. Never send money to someone who asks online – even a good friend, and especially an acquaintance or stranger.

2. Don't send money to people who say they need it to get out of jail, or say they are lost in another country or need money to pay for a doctor or operation. This is a rule ALWAYS ... even if they sound like they really need it and you feel sorry for them, don't send them money. Remember people lie online and they lie very well.

3. Don't give your possessions to people who ask for them on-line. For example, there is no reason to send someone your newest video game so they can try it out.

Buying Things

- Just because you see a product on TV or online, it doesn't mean it is a good thing for you to buy.

- If someone advertises that their mixer sells for $300 but you can have it for $29.95, they are most likely lying. It is either junk or stolen.

- The rules for budgeting and shopping that you follow when you go to a store also apply to online shopping. Decide what you want to buy, budget for it, and then research the best place to buy it.

- On a lot of sites, and in many games, you can make in-site purchases. You need to budget for them also. If you want the sword that will get you to level 50 in your favorite game, don't spend the bus money you need to get to work.

- Don't buy anything impulsively – think it through first.

- If you are going to buy anything online, register with a third-party payer like PayPal (paypal.com). This way you won't be giving your credit card number to lots of sellers.

- If you're under 18, check with your parents before you buy anything online.

Watch out for Online Scams

The following is only a partial list of scams you might encounter. People are coming up with new ones all of the time.

- Be careful when you sign up for online subscription services. Reputable ones like Netflix and Amazon Prime post clear guidelines on their websites. Subscriptions that are not reputable may be very hard to get out of once you sign on. If you feel you must subscribe, make sure you know how to cancel before you commit.

- Be wary of anything that offers you stuff for free if you buy things later (like CDs or magazines). You will probably end up paying more for the items, and the free ones won't really be free.

- Any organization that tells you that you'll make a lot of money working at home if you send them money to join their service is lying to you. Don't send them the registration fee. Real online jobs don't ask you to pay first.

- Anyone who says if you invest with them they will guarantee to double or triple your money is lying. Don't send them your money. Honest financial advisors will meet you in real life, in a real office.

The basic rule when it comes to scams is: **IF IT SOUNDS TOO GOOD TO BE TRUE, IT IS TOO GOOD TO BE TRUE!**

Cyberbullying

Just as you can be bullied or be a bully in person, there are bullies online. This is known as cyberbullying. Cyberbullying includes …

- Threatening people in online posts or messages

- Saying hurtful things or calling people names

- Sharing someone's personal information or photos with others in order to embarrass them or make fun of them

- Extorting money or possessions. Saying you need to give the bully something to stay safe

- Spreading rumors about someone

- Saying anything mean about someone's race, age group, looks, gender, or sexual orientation

- Creating an online group or page to deliberately exclude someone

If an online "friend" cyberbullies you, "unfriend" him and report him to the administrator of your social networking site. Most sites have instructions on how to do this; if not, use the "contact us" section to send an email to the site administrator. If you live with your parents, tell them you're being bullied online. Ask if you should call the police. If you don't live with your parents, you should still tell them, or a teacher, counselor, or social skills coach. Any of these people can either help you or direct you to someone who can help.

REMEMBER

1. Don't be a cyberbully.

2. Don't do things that are illegal.

- You may think you're being cool and "trash talking," but if you repeatedly say mean and hurtful things to people online you are cyberbullying.

- If you threaten someone, that is called *assault*.

- If you spread rumors about someone, that is called *slander*.

- If you demand things with a promise not to spread rumors, that is called *extortion*.

- Constantly sending online messages to someone who doesn't reply is called *harassment*.

All of these acts are punishable by law. Don't do them! If somebody does any of these acts to you, tell a person in authority, like a parent, teacher, or counselor.

Another area in which lots of danger lurks online is romance and sex. This area is so important that we are going to devote the next two chapters to discussing the rules of romance and sex.

Chapter 5

ROMANCE AND SEX

IN PERSON

Online social networking sites can be a wonderful place for you to practice all kinds of interactions, including interactions with the kind of people you might be interested in romantically. But those interactions also have the greatest potential for getting you into trouble – SERIOUS TROUBLE, GO-TO-PRISON-TYPE OF TROUBLE – if you don't know and follow the rules.

Before we can talk about romance and sex online, we need to talk about how these things work in person. We'll talk about romance first. Like friendship, there are levels of relationships in this area. But before we can introduce the types of romantic relationships, we need to talk a bit about flirting, because flirting plays a role in many romantic interactions.

Flirting

Flirting is a complicated social activity with many variations. People flirt all the time, but it doesn't necessarily mean they want a romantic relationship or a sexual relationship. In the more detailed explanation later in this chapter, we call people who do this with each other just for fun "flirt buddies." For them, flirting can just be another way of being friendly.

But flirting is also how people let each other know that they are interested in romantic or sexual relationships with each other.

It is very important that you know what your intentions are when you flirt with others and that you understand what is being offered when someone flirts with you.

Warning: Improper flirting will get you in trouble – whether you do it in person or online.

To make this a little easier to understand, we will explain some of the behaviors that are part of flirting.

Making Eye Contact

In the real world, eye contact is very significant. Looking into someone's eyes briefly but repeatedly as you talk with them shows that you are interested in what they are saying. Holding eye contact for a little longer can be a way of flirting. Looking at a person's eyes for too long may be considered staring or aggressive, and that makes people uncomfortable.

It is difficult to give a rule about timing with eye contact. Just remember that it is not good to stare. However, it is also not good to avoid eye contact altogether.

Body Language

People flirt with one another by smiling suggestively or by touching each other in a casual way. Examples include touching someone's arm as you talk or putting an arm around their shoulders when you walk with them or sit next to them at a movie or restaurant. People also stand closer to people they are flirting with or are romantically involved with than they do to other people.

Verbal Flirting

This can involve flattering the person with exaggerated compliments (for example, "you're the cutest guy in class"). This type of flirting can also consist of laughing together about a funny experience you shared. It can also involve using words to show you like the other person. For example, if a group is going to a pizza restaurant, you can say to the person you're flirting with "Would you like to sit next to me?" After such an interchange, you can smile together or laugh.

Trying to Get Attention

People can flirt by arranging to encounter the person they are interested in romantically (for example, showing up near the person's locker between classes). They can also write the person notes, give her small gifts, or dress up to look attractive and noticeable. Offering tastes of your food in a group-eating situation is another flirting behavior that falls in this category.

Warning! Flirting is tricky. There is a fine line between flirting and stalking or harassing. Here are some differences.

Flirting	Stalking or Harassing
Trying to get attention by hanging out (once or twice) at the locker or desk of someone you like romantically	Hanging out by someone's locker or desk every day or multiple times in one day (without being asked to do so) is stalking.
Flirting verbally by leaving one or two friendly messages on someone's voicemail	Continuing to leave lots of voicemail messages if you haven't gotten a return call with a friendly message is stalking. Don't tell yourself that the other person is just too busy to call back yet and that you should keep trying. The online version of this is sending a lot of messages or "friend" requests without getting a response.
Trying to get attention by writing someone you like a note that contains a compliment	If you don't get a verbal or written response that is also a compliment after writing more than one note of this kind, you are annoying and may be harassing the person you are writing to.
Trying to get attention by offering someone you like romantically a taste of your food in a group-eating situation	Continuing to offer food "tastes" or treats to a person you like romantically, without getting a friendly response and offers back is annoying and can be interpreted as harassing.
Trying to get attention by wearing especially attractive clothing (once or twice) when you know you will be seeing the person you like	Dressing up every time you see the person and asking him if you look nice so he will notice and say something about how you look is annoying and can be harassing.
Flirting verbally by telling someone (once or twice) that she looks especially pretty today	Complimenting someone every time you see her or telling her she is "hot" and you want to kiss her or have sex with her is harassment. You can get in trouble with the law.
Using body language by touching someone's arm (once or twice) briefly when you chat with them	Touching someone constantly when you talk with them, or standing so close to them that you make them uncomfortable is harassing. You will know they are uncomfortable if they move away from you.

Reading this section will help you understand some of the different ways in which people flirt. But flirting is complicated, so you may need coaching to figure out the techniques and rules of flirting. Talk to someone you trust for advice.

In general, there are two good rules to follow when it comes to flirting:

1. If someone doesn't flirt back after you've flirted with them three times, assume they are not interested in you and move on to someone else. If you keep flirting with them you are stalking or harassing them.

2. NEVER, EVER flirt with a teacher, boss, police officer, or any person who is in a position of authority. It is always inappropriate.

Romantic Relationships

Now that we've talked about flirting, we can introduce the romantic relationship categories. They include the following.

Crushes

Crushes are people you are attracted to, but with whom you are not going to have a real relationship. For example, you can have a crush on a teacher, a celebrity, or the captain of the football team. You admire a crush from afar and maybe you daydream about him or her. You do not do anything to promote a real relationship, and you do not flirt with crushes.

Flirt Buddies

These are friends of the opposite gender (or the same gender if that is your preference). There may be a bit of a mutual attraction, but **neither person is expecting the relationship to become a romance or become sexual.** With these buddies, the flirting is mostly verbal. It is not okay to ask someone to be a flirt buddy because we made up the term and people won't know what you're talking about. If you aren't sure, just treat someone as a good friend, and don't flirt with him or her.

People You Flirt With Seriously

These are people you know or meet whom you find attractive. You want a romantic or sexual relationship with them, so you use flirting behavior to let them know you are interested. Serious flirting can be verbal, but it can also involve dressing in a special way to get attention or approval, or being more careful with your grooming in order to be attractive. You can also use eye contact and some of the body language flirting behaviors we listed earlier.

People You See Romantically

If you flirt with someone and he or she flirts back, at some point you will want to ask the person out, or he or she may ask you out. This isn't just a "guy thing." A girl is free to ask a guy out if he's been flirting with her and she likes it. Once this happens, the relationship moves into the category of People You See Romantically. These are people you go out with on dates, or if you are out with a group, the two of you walk and sit together and are seen as a couple. You are attracted to each other, and you enjoy spending time together. But you have no commitment to each other, and you are both free to date other people, too.

Boyfriends or Girlfriends

When you've dated someone for a while, he or she may become your boyfriend or girlfriend. This process can be tricky because there is no rule about when someone crosses the line from being a person you date to becoming a boyfriend or girlfriend. If you are boyfriend and girlfriend, it means you will no longer date other people. Everyone has trouble knowing when this line has been crossed, so ask if you aren't sure. But you have to be prepared to accept the answer you get if it is "No." If someone isn't ready for that commitment with you, don't get angry or act out.

More Serious Romance Partners

This category includes people who are "in love." BEING IN LOVE IS MUTUAL – IT INVOLVES BOTH PARTIES. Some serious romance partners become engaged and plan to marry each other. People who are already married to each other also belong to this category.

Meeting People in Person

How do you meet people you can have romantic relationships with in real life? There are several ways, including …

- Many people meet romance partners at work or school.

- You can meet romance partners in activities based on your special interests, like joining clubs or taking classes.

- Some people who are over 21 go to bars or nightclubs in order to meet romance partners.

- Some people introduce friends to other friends they think might be suitable romance partners for them. Going out with someone like this without knowing him or her beforehand is called a "blind date."

- Some adults who are over 21 put personal ads in magazines, newspapers, or special online dating services, mentioning things about themselves and listing what they are looking for in a partner. The good thing about these services is that there is no ambiguity about the goal. Both persons are involved because they are looking for partners, and the dating sites have rules that let you know when someone wants to date you. For example, the site may only send you information about people who have expressed an interest in your profile.

Physical Contact and Sex

Romance can be tricky, but physical contact and sex can be even trickier, because people have different rules about what is okay to do within different categories of relationships, and how old someone should be before they consider being sexual with other people.

Some people feel that a couple should be married or at least be serious romance partners before they have sex with each other, but they think kissing or even sexual touching that doesn't lead to intercourse is okay in more casual relationships.

Other people feel that it is okay to have sex once you are officially boyfriend and girlfriend. Still others feel that it is okay to have sex with someone you know very casually, as long as both people agree and don't have another boyfriend or girlfriend, fiancé, or spouse.

It is also okay not to have sex with a boyfriend or girlfriend, but some kinds of touching are usually part of the relationship. Examples include holding hands, kissing, putting yours arms around each other, hugging, touching, fixing the other person's hair, or straightening your partner's collar.

We can't tell you which of these choices is right for you, but if you are over 18, we suggest you talk to a caring adult like a parent or a therapist before you decide and that you NEVER do anything physical or sexual with someone else that makes them or you uncomfortable.

If you are under 18, do not date or have a boyfriend or girlfriend without the knowledge and consent of your parents. It is also important that you talk to your parents about their sexual values and what they expect your sexually related behavior to be. You can also discuss these issues with another trusted adult, like a therapist or counselor.

Two rules are extremely important when it comes to physical contact and sex. Failure to follow these rules can have VERY serious consequences, like going to prison and being labeled a sex offender.

1. **ANY** kind of sexual contact or sexual talk **MUST** be consensual. "Consensual" means you both agree. If someone says no, they mean no. They don't mean keep trying. Consensual sex means having only as much physical or sexual contact as

BOTH partners want. It doesn't matter if you want to have sex. If the other person does not, it means **STOP** when they ask you to. **IMMEDIATELY.**

2. Every state has laws against having sex with people who are considered too young, even if they consent. **The age limit varies from state to state. It is important to know what the law is in your state and to honor it.** Failure to do so is called "statutory rape." It is a crime, even if both people agree to be sexual with each other.

   And here is a third thing we'll mention but not discuss in detail.

3. If you are sexually active, protect yourself and your partner from pregnancy and sexually transmitted diseases. Guys, use a condom. Girls, be sure to get an effective method of birth control from your doctor and use it, and don't have sex with a guy who doesn't use a condom. If a guy refuses to use a condom, it means he doesn't care about the welfare of the person he's having sex with.

Chapter 6
ROMANCE AND SEX ONLINE

Now we are ready to talk about romance and sex online. Let's start by talking about the categories of romantic relationships that we introduced in the last chapter.

Types of Romantic Relationships

Crushes

You can have a crush on a celebrity you follow on Twitter or a person you find attractive who agrees to be an online "friend" but who is really an acquaintance. (See Chapter 2 for the definition of an acquaintance.) The same rules apply to online crushes as to in-person crushes. You can watch from afar, but **do not** initiate any contact.

Flirt Buddies

In an online game or chat room, you may meet people you like talking to and enjoy flirting with using the verbal flirting techniques in written form. These people are online flirt buddies. This is fine to do, as long as you both participate in the flirting behavior.

People You Flirt With Seriously

If you play an online game, go to chat rooms, or belong to online groups, you might meet someone you are interested in as a romance partner. If you have had at least three friendly back-and-forth exchanges with the person and you want to find out if he or she is romantically inclined towards you, you can try some mild flirting. Things that are okay to do include:

- **Compliments:** For example, telling the person how nice he or she looks in the photos posted online; that he or she is beautiful or handsome.

- **Flattering:** Complimenting someone in an exaggerated way is flattery. Like saying somebody is the best player in the game you both play or SO smart, or hilariously funny when they tell a joke.

- **Poking:** When you "poke" someone on Facebook, they get a message telling them that they have been "poked." Some people consider this flirting, but others say this is just a way to be friendly. (We introduced the rules for poking in Chapter 3. Excessive poking can be a form of stalking.)

- **Sending an online "gift":** These are virtual, not real, items that usually cost a small amount of money to send. When you send these gifts, the recipient will receive a message on his or her webpage and a graphic that represents the gift.

REMEMBER

If you do any online flirting three times and the other person doesn't respond by initiating any flirting with you, **STOP.** They are not interested in you in that way.

Boyfriends and Girlfriends

You might meet someone online and find you like each other a lot. You may chat together every day. You may play online games together all of the time. The feelings appear to be mutual. You may even call each other "girlfriend" or "boyfriend," even though you only communicate online. It is okay to be romantic in this way as long as it is mutual.

Do not have a more intimate relationship than this with someone online. Online relationships become a problem if they become sexual in any way.

REMEMBER

The rule about online sex is: DON'T DO IT.

Almost every type of online sexual communication is dangerous or illegal. This includes:

- Sexting (sending sexually suggestive text messages to people). This includes any mention of a sexual act you would like to do with the person or a comment about the sexual parts of her body, like her breasts

- Posting sexually suggestive or nude photos or videos or sending them to people directly

- Looking at or sharing sexually suggestive photos of nude children

- Emailing sexually explicit or suggestive messages

- Talking about private body parts in any way

- Posting "dirty" jokes

Only have sexual relationships with people you know in person. Remember, if you are thinking about having online sex with a person because he or she looks cute in the profile picture, he or she may not be real. That cute 19-year-old boy may really be a smelly 50-year-old guy who is drinking a beer as he talks to you. That cute 20-year-old girl may be 75 years old with mild dementia. That so-called 20-year-old girl may not even be a girl!

Meeting in Person

This leads us to another important point. What do you do if you meet someone online whom you want to meet in person?

Be very, very, very careful here. Remember what we said above and in Chapter 1 about people's online persona. Some people lie. The Internet is a place where many predatory people lurk, hoping to find people to take advantage of.

Despite all this, if you still feel you just have to meet someone in person, don't do it without taking precautions. Here are some things to do to keep you safe.

- Meet during the day in a public place like a restaurant, coffee shop, or library. That way, if the person you are meeting turns out to be someone you're uncomfortable with, you can leave easily.

- Bring a friend, family member, or trusted professional with you when you meet your online "friend" in person for the first time.

- If someone can't come with you, at least make sure that someone knows what you're doing and where you're going.

- Don't share personal information like your address with an online "friend" before you meet in person. Don't even share this information at your first in-person meeting.

The meeting could be a disaster, but it could also be that the person is what you thought and you both like each other. You may want to see each other more. There are things you both like and you talk about doing some of them together. Congratulations! If that happens, you now have the beginnings of a real in-person relationship, not just an online one.

You can continue to see the person, but be cautious about sharing personal information or being physically intimate. When you first meet in person, treat your friend like an acquaintance or gaming buddy. As you spend more time together and build trust in the course of several in-person meetings, you can start to relate to her as a good friend or even a best friend, girlfriend, or sex partner ... so long as the decision to share confidences or physical contact is mutual – both parties must agree!

There is one more thing we have to tell you about – your online relationship status. Failure to understand the social rules here can also get you in trouble. Not legal trouble, but trouble with your friends or your romance partners.

Your Online Relationship Status

Some social networking sites have a place where you can identify your online relationship status as a way to let others know whether or not you are in a romantic relationship and what your preferences are in this area. You can change your status whenever you want, and you can say whatever you want about your status. It is important not to give too much information.

It is okay to say that ...

- You are single and interested in a relationship

- You are straight, gay, or transgender – as long as you want people to know this information

- You are in a committed relationship – if you have a mutually agreed upon boyfriend or girlfriend relationship with someone

- You are engaged or married, if that is true

It is not okay to say …

- Whether or not you are a virgin

- What kinds of physical activities you want to do with a partner

- That you are lonely or horny

You also should never use your online relationship status as a way of communicating with a real or potential romantic partner.

- Don't say you are in a relationship with someone if you aren't. Do your communicating directly with the person. Then post a status that tells the truth.

- Don't tell a partner you are mad at him or her through your relationship status.

- Don't break up with someone by changing your relationship status. If you are in a relationship and you want to end it, do it directly and nicely. Breaking up by changing your status to "available" is mean, and people who do it are jerks. **DON'T DO IT**.

Chapter 7

TO SUM UP

In this chapter we will summarize some things we covered earlier and add a few more ideas for you to think about. **You may be tempted to skip the other chapters and just read this one. Don't do that.** We're going to be very general here, and it is important that you read the details that are presented in the other chapters if you want to understand the rules of social networking, both in person and online.

The Rules

Rule #1:

If you use a social networking website, create an online persona or profile that represents your best self.

Rule #2:

Understanding the different types of friends and how to communicate with each type in person will help you if you want to interact with "friends" online.

Rule #3:

In-person friendships are two-way. If you are doing all of the work, it is not a friendship. The same is true of online friendships.

Rule #4:

Friends are nice to each other and respect each other. If someone is mean, insulting, or abusive to you, he or she is not a friend.

Rule #5:

Someone who would be categorized as an acquaintance or total stranger in real life can be an online "friend."

Rule #6:

Don't let yourself be bullied, and don't be a bully, either in person or online. It's against the law in most places.

Rule #7:

Be very careful about what you say or post online. The Internet is forever, and even if you thought you deleted something, it can still exist somewhere online.

Rule #8:

Tell the truth online, but avoid TMI (giving **T**oo **M**uch **I**nformation). You may be fascinated with the details of your special interests and activities, but others may not. This is also true when you interact in person.

Rule #9:

Always protect yourself from predatory people and online scams.

Rule #10:

Never share personal or financial information online – whether it is your information or other people's.

Rule #11:

If you want to get involved in online romances, know and follow the rules and remember that many people lie about themselves online.

Rule #12:

Sometimes it is okay to flirt, but it is never okay to stalk or harass people (in person or online).

Rule #13:

It is NEVER a good idea to do or say anything sexual online or to use curse words.

Rule #14:

Never, ever meet someone in person whom you first encountered online without taking precautions. If you are under 18, you must let an adult like a parent know what you are planning to do. If you are over 18, let a counselor or social skills coach know.

Back to In-Person Relationships

Online social networking can have a wonderful place in your life, but it should never be your whole life. Online relating is good because you can control the speed and content of the interactions. That is helpful when you are trying out being social. After you practice relating to others online for a while, you may feel more comfortable and ready to test out your relationship skills in person. If so, you can try some of the following:

- Try being your best self in your everyday life, not just on-line. Dress a little nicer and pay a little more attention to your grooming. Think, would I want a picture of the way I look now to be online where everyone can see it? If the answer is "yes," you're presenting yourself in a way that represents your best self.

- Get some exercise. Sitting in front of a computer all day isn't good for anyone. A health club or a Y where you exercise is another place where you can make friends. Also, if you work out, you'll look and feel better.

- If you aren't in school, take a class or join a club that meets in person, not online. Even if you don't meet people, you can learn things that you will find fun and interesting.

- Use the categories in this guide to help you think about and work on your existing relationships. Is there someone who is an acquaintance, but you wish he or she was a good friend? Think about things you could do to get closer. Ask someone you trust for advice.

- Use what you learned about your online "friends" to initiate conversations with them in person. For example, if you have an acquaintance from school or work and you learn online that he has a favorite band, the next time you see him, start a conversation about that band's music.

A Final Note

No one is perfect at making and keeping relationships. We all make mistakes and we all learn as we go. But as long as you know and follow the secret rules of social networking, you will not do things that could hurt other people or yourself, and you can have relationships that are fun and rewarding.

Chapter 8

WANT TO READ MORE?

If you're interested in reading other books about social networking, we've listed a few that you might try. You don't need to read these to learn the secret rules. But you may want to get more information or see what other people are writing about this topic. Some of these books were written for teens; others for adults. Some are aimed at parents, but that doesn't mean that other people can't read them, too. You can probably find many of these books at your local library.

"Cautionary Tales"

These books tell a story to let you know about some of the bad things that can happen when people don't follow the secret rules.

A Girl's Life Online by Katherine Tarbox (Perfection Learning, 2004) This is true story about a 13-year-old girl who met an older man in a chat room, then agreed to meet him in person. The girl wrote the book when she was 18.

Top 8: Book 1 (series) by Katie Finn (Point, 2008) This fiction series is about a popular high school student and her friends, and relating online is a big part of the story. In the first book, her profile on a made-up social networking site called Friendverse is hacked. Other books in the series include *What's Your Status?* and *Unfriended.*

Want to Go Private? by Sarah Darer Littman (Scholastic Press, 2011)
In this novel for teens, a girl develops an online boyfriend/girlfriend relationship. She doesn't tell her family about it, and it turns out that the boy is not who or what she thought he was.

Informational Books, Not Stories

Friend Me! 600 Years of Social Networking in America by Francesca Davis DiPiazza (21st Century, 2012)
This book introduces ways that people connected before computers were invented; for example, using telegrams. It also discusses social networking online.

How Not to Be a Dick: An Everyday Etiquette Guide by Meghan Doherty (Zest Books, 2013)
In a style that is silly at times, the author presents useful information about social rules. This guide was written primarily for adolescents and young adults.

I Know Who You Are and I Saw What You Did: Social Networks and the Death of Privacy by Lori Andrews (Free Press, 2012)
This book explores the legal and constitutional rights of social media users and discusses problems people have experienced because of things they have posted online.

Lol ... OMG!: What Every Student Needs to Know About Online Reputation Management, Digital Citizenship and Cyberbullying by Matt Ivester (CreateSpace Independent Publishing Platform, 2011)
This book starts out presenting real cases to demonstrate the potential negative consequences of common online behaviors. The author then suggests ways that high school and college students can be more responsible users of social media.

The Parent's Guide to Texting, Facebook and Social Media: Understanding the Benefits and Dangers of Parenting in a Digital World by Shawn Marie Edgington (Brown Books Publishing Group, 2011)
This book was written by an expert in cyberbullying prevention to

give parents the information they need to help their teenage children stay safe online.

Books Written by and for People With ASD

If you are a person with ASD and would like to read more that can help you understand real-world social behavior, you may want to try these.

The Aspie Teen's Survival Guide: Candid Advice for Teens, Tweens, and Parents, From a Young Man with Asperger's Syndrome by J. D. Kraus (Future Horizons, 2010)
Based on his own experience, the author gives advice on how to succeed in middle and high school, covering topics such as bullying, socializing and friendship, and dating and relationships.

Autism-Asperger's and Sexuality: Puberty and Beyond by Jerry Newport and Mary Newport (Future Horizons, 2002)
In this book, a married couple, both of whom have ASD, talk candidly about romance and sex. They provide information from the point of view of both partners in the relationship.

Autistics' Guide to Dating: A Book by Autistics, for Autistics and Those Who Love Them or Who Are in Love With Them by Emilia Murry Ramey and Jody John Ramey (Jessica Kingsley, 2008)
Sensory skills deficits and sensory processing problems can create barriers to dating success for people with ASD. The authors of this book offer strategies that can help overcome these difficulties.

Unwritten Rules of Social Relationships: Decoding Social Mysteries Through the Unique Perspectives of Autism by Dr. Temple Grandin and Sean Barron (Future Horizons, 2005)
Two people with ASD share the rules of in-person social relationships that they discovered through their own life experiences. Some of their rules are the same as the ones in this book and some cover areas we didn't address.

This book will help you understand some behaviors that could get you in trouble:

A 5 is Against the Law! Social Boundaries: Straight Up! An Honest Guide for Teens and Young Adults by Kari Dunn Buron (AAPC, 2007)
This book takes a look at behaviors that can spell trouble for adolescents and young adults who have difficulty understanding and maintaining social boundaries. To avoid getting into trouble, the reader is encouraged to think about and create his own behavior on an anxiety scale that applies to his particular emotions and situations.

Related Titles

A 5 Is Against the Law! Social Boundaries: Straight Up! An honest guide for teens and young adults

by Kari Dunn Buron, MS

This book builds on the popular *The Incredible 5-Point Scale*. It takes a narrower look at challenging behavior with a particular focus on behaviors that can spell trouble for adolescents and young adults who have difficulty understanding and maintaining social boundaries. Speaking directly to adolescents and young adults, a section of the book is devoted to how to cope with anxiety before it begins to escalate, often leading to impulsive and unacceptable behavior.

ISBN 9781931282352 | Code 9975 | Price: $20.95

Diary of a Social Detective
Real-Life Tales of Mystery, Intrigue and Interpersonal Adventure

by Jeffrey E. Jessum, PhD

Foremost a detective/mystery story for readers ages 8 and older, this book delivers insights, tools and solutions in an engaging storyline that kids can relate to. It is recommended not just for individual kids needing social skills tools, but on a broader basis for all kids wanting to read something interesting and fun. Cleverly developed chapters allow readers to use their own social detective skills to solve the mysteries.

ISBN 9781934575710 | Code 9063 | Price: $19.95

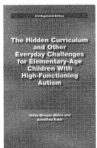

Social Rules for Kids
The Top 100 Social Rules Kids Need to Succeed

by Sue Diamond, MA, CCC

Social Rules for Kids helps open the door of communication between parent and child by addressing 100 social rules for home, school and the community. Written directly to the student, these clear rules cover topics such as body language, manners and feelings. Reminders of appropriate social rules at the end of each page are combined into a complete list for easy reference.

ISBN 9781934575840 | Code 9067 | Price: $19.95

The Hidden Curriculum and Other Everyday Challenges for Elementary-Age Children With High-Functioning Autism

by Haley Morgan Myles and Annellise Kolar

In this 2nd expanded edition, previously entitled *Practical Solutions to Everyday Challenges for Children with Asperger Syndrome*, young authors Haley Myles and Annellise Kolar give simple, no-nonsense advice on how to handle everyday occurrences that can be challenging for children on the autism spectrum. This reader-friendly book provides social rules that help children with peer relationships, school and everyday activities.

ISBN 9781937473105 | Code 9917 | Price: $14.95

To order, please visit www.aapcpublishing.net

From AAPC

The Hidden Curriculum for Understanding Unstated Rules in Social Situations for Adolescents and Young Adults

by Brenda Smith Myles, PhD, Melissa L. Trautman, MsEd, and Ronda L. Schelvan, MsEd; foreword by Michelle Garcia Winner

In the revised and expanded edition of this book, the authors narrow their target to issues common to adolescents and young adults. While many of the features of the original book have been maintained, information on evidence-based practice has been added. Further, a series of instructional strategies are provided that can be used to teach the hidden curriculum.

ISBN 9781937473747 | Code 9942A | Price: $19.95

Social Behavior and Self-Management: 5-Point Scales for Adolescents and Adults

by Kari Dunn Buron, MS, Jane Thierfeld Brown, EdD, Mitzi Curtis, MA, and Lisa King, MEd

Building on the success on the almost legendary *Incredible 5-Point Scale* by Buron and Curtis, this book also uses scales as a way of explaining social and emotional concepts to individuals who have difficulty understanding such information but have a relative strength in understanding systems.

ISBN 9781934575918 | Code 9101 | Price: $19.95

The Guide to Dating for Teenagers With Asperger Syndrome

by Jeannie Uhlenkamp

Written in a question-and-answer format, this much-needed resource offers insight and practical advice on dating challenges for teens with Asperger Syndrome, who often struggle with social issues. Each topic is followed by discussion questions designed to get conversations flowing between teens, parents and teachers with the main point succinctly identified for each topic.

ISBN 9781934575536 | Code 9041 | Price: $19.95

Asperger Download: A Guide to Help Teenage Males With Asperger Syndrome Trouble-Shoot Life's Challenges

by Josie and Damian Santomauro

Being a teenager is an experience simultaneously shared by teens and their parents. In this book, Damian Santomauro and his mother, Josie Santomauro, share their dual experiences by defining major terms that teenage males encounter during their journey into manhood. Damian Santomauro was diagnosed with Asperger Syndrome at the age of 5. Now he's in college and ready to share his experiences with teens who are experiencing what he lived through. Appropriate for teenage males ages 11-16.

ISBN 9781934575024 | Code 9990 | Price: $19.95

11209 Strang Line Rd.
Lenexa, Kansas 66215
www.aapcpublishing.net

CPSIA information can be obtained at www.ICGtesting.com
Printed in the USA
LVOW04s0831270315

432282LV00002B/4/P